WITHDRAWN

Transportation

by Sally Hewitt

amicus

Published by Amicus
P.O. Box 1329, Mankato, Minnesota 56002

Printed in the United States of America at Corporate Graphics, in North Mankato, Minnesota.

Published by arrangement with the Watts Publishing Group Ltd., London.

Library of Congress Cataloging-in-Publication Data

Hewitt, Sally, 1949-
  Transportation / by Sally Hewitt.
     p. cm. -- (Starting geography)
  Includes index.
  Summary: "Discusses different types of transportation, how they are used, and where each type can be found. Includes hands-on activities"--Provided by publisher.
  ISBN 978-1-60753-129-6 (library binding)
  1. Transportation--Juvenile literature. 2. Travel--Juvenile literature. I. Title.
  HE152.H492 2011
  388--dc22
                                        2009053175

Editor: Katie Dicker
Art Direction: Rahul Dhiman (Q2AMedia)
Designer: Shruti Aggarwal (Q2AMedia)
Picture researcher: Ekta Sharma, and Debabrata Sen (Q2AMedia)
Craft models made by: Tarang Saggar (Q2AMedia)
Photography: Tarang Saggar (Q2AMedia)

1211
32010

Picture credits:
t=top b=bottom c=center l=left r=right

Cover: Shutterstock
Title page: Cenk Unver/Dreamstime
Insides: Günter Lenz/Photolibrary: 6, Steve Vidler/Photolibrary: 7t, Masterfile: 7b, Kristi Torsak/Istockphoto: 8t, Stuart Howarth/Istockphoto: 8b, Mike Norton/Fotolia: 9bl, Greg Larson/Istockphoto: 9br, Jo Yong Hak/Reuters: 10, Robert Wisdom/Dreamstime: 12t, Young Kimpark/Dreamstime: 12b, Cenk Unver/Dreamstime: 14t, Photowitch/Dreamstime: 14b, Rostislav Glinsky/Dreamstime: 16, Bedfordshire County Council: 18t, Japan Travel Bureau/Photolibrary: 18b, Lim Wui Liang/The Straits Times/Contributor/Getty Images: 20t, Javier Larrea/Photolibrary: 20b, Stepanov/Can Stock Photo: 21, Peter Titmuss/Alamy: 22, Jacek Chabraszewski/Istockphoto: 23, Jose Fuste Raga/Photolibrary: 24t, Gene Chutka/Istockphoto: 24b, Masterfile: 26, Masterfile: 27.
Q2AMedia Image Bank: Cover, Imprint page, 13, 15, 17, 19.
Q2AMedia Art Bank: Contents page, 9, 11, 13, 15, 17, 19, 25, 27.

With thanks to our models Shruti Aggarwal and Nazia Zaidi.

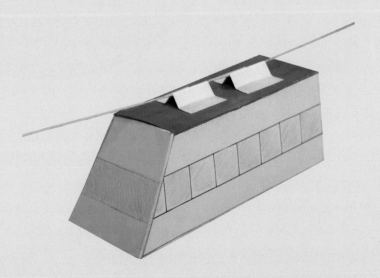

Contents

Words that appear in **bold** can be found in the glossary on pages 28–29.

What Is Transportation?

Transportation is the carrying of people and **goods** from place to place in vehicles. Trains, trucks, vans, cars, and bicycles all carry people and goods on land. Boats travel over water and aircraft fly across the skies.

Wheels and Engines

Vehicles on wheels pulled by horses or mules have been used for thousands of years to transport people and heavy goods. Tracks and roads were built for the wheels to run on. Today, many vehicles have powerful engines that run on fuel. They carry enormous loads and lots of people.

Truck drivers fill their trucks with fuel at gas stations. Gasoline or diesel gives engines the power to work.

Pedal Power

Bicycles were invented about 200 years ago. They are cheap to use because they don't need fuel, just strong legs to push the pedals and turn the wheels. Bicycles are good for traveling short distances.

In China, many people bike to work.

This family is looking at vacation brochures to plan a trip away.

A Small World

Modern transportation has made it possible for people to travel all over the world faster and more cheaply than ever before. A trip from the U.S. to Europe used to take a few weeks by boat. Now it can be done in about 12 hours by airplane. When people travel to far away places, they learn about the traditions and ways of life in a different country.

Roads and Bridges

Land vehicles need roads to drive on. Highways cross countries and continents, and roads link towns and cities. Small roads wind through the countryside, too.

Tunnels

Mountains, rivers, **gorges**, and the sea create natural barriers for **traffic** traveling along roads. Tunnels take traffic through mountains or under gorges, rivers, and the sea to cross these barriers by the shortest route.

Driving through a tunnel in the mountains makes a journey quicker.

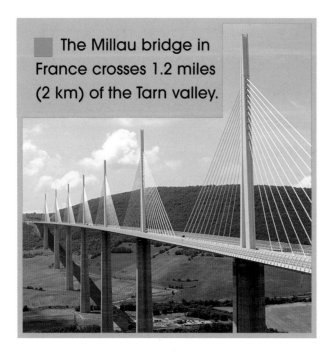

The Millau bridge in France crosses 1.2 miles (2 km) of the Tarn valley.

Bridges

Bridges carry vehicles across rivers, valleys, gorges, and water. They have to carry the weight of the traffic and stay standing in high winds. Bridges made with stone and iron look solid and strong. Today, modern **materials** make strong bridges that look delicate.

Make a Model Bridge

Design a bridge that doesn't spoil the scenery it crosses.

You will need:
- two large sheets of card stock • pencil • paints
- corrugated cardboard
- scissors • glue
- fine silver string

1 On one sheet of card stock, draw and paint a river valley.

2 Design your own bridge to cross the valley. Look in books and on the Internet for ideas. You could build a bridge with stone arches or pillars, or a suspension bridge with cables, for example.

3 Cut out the parts of your bridge from card stock and cardboard. Paint the parts to look like stone, concrete, or metal, and arrange them across your valley scene. You could cut the silver string to make some "cables" to stick on.

How can you make the colors and shape of your bridge blend in with the surroundings?

Long-Distance Trucks

Trucks carry goods over long distances.
They carry materials to factories and take
items made in factories to shops to be sold.
Refrigerated trucks keep food cool and fresh.

Driving Safely

Trucks are the biggest
vehicles on the road. On
the highway, they keep
to the outside lanes so that
smaller, faster vehicles can
pass them. Big side mirrors
show drivers what is going
on around them. Lights
flash and warnings sound
when a truck backs up.

Crossing Borders

Sometimes, long-distance
trucks cross continents.
They pass **border controls**
when they drive through
different countries. Border
control officers check
passports and the goods
the vehicles are carrying.

These trucks are being
checked before they drive
across a border.

Choose a Long-Distance Truck Route

Choose a route for a truck carrying wood to a factory.

You will need:
• large sheet of card stock or paper • pencil • markers
• string • scissors • poster putty

1 Copy the map shown below onto the large piece of card stock or paper.

2 Use the string to find the length of each route. Stick one end of the string to the lumber yard with the poster putty.

Now lay the string along the road following the twists and turns. Cut the end of the string when you reach the factory. Repeat for all routes.

3 Compare the length of the pieces of string. If 1 in. = 10 mi., how long is each route? If 1 cm = 10 km, how long is each route? Which is the longest?

Make a chart like the one below, and then decide which route you would take.

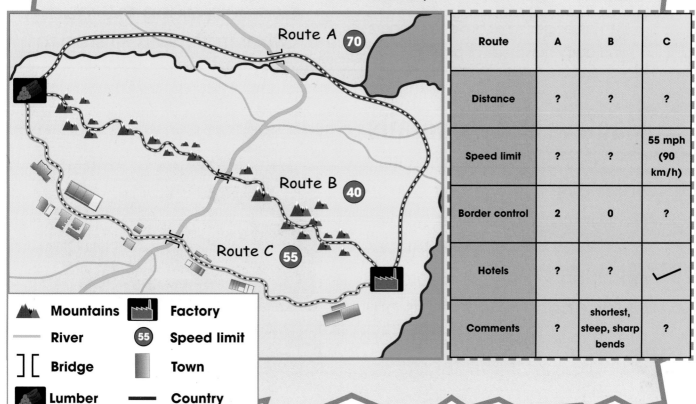

Route A 70
Route B 40
Route C 55

Route	A	B	C
Distance	?	?	?
Speed limit	?	?	55 mph (90 km/h)
Border control	2	0	?
Hotels	?	?	✓
Comments	?	shortest, steep, sharp bends	?

Mountains **Factory**

River **55 Speed limit**

Bridge **Town**

Lumber yard **Country border**

Traveling on Tracks

Trains pulled by a **locomotive** run on railroad tracks that cross countries all over the world. Trains are powered by **diesel** or **electricity** and can carry many passengers.

Passenger trains have lots of cars and carry hundreds of people.

Trains and Trams

As well as trains over land, many big cities have an underground subway system. Trains pass through tunnels that run beneath busy city streets. Trams are like buses that run quickly on tracks along the road. Other traffic has to stop to give trams the right-of-way.

Maglevs and Monorails

Maglevs and monorails are trains that run without burning diesel. Maglevs hover above a rail and move smoothly and silently using the force of **magnetism**. Monorails are electric trains that hang from a single rail above them.

This maglev in Australia moves people quickly into the city.

Make a Monorail Cab

You will need:
- 2 sheets of white card stock
- pencil • ruler • markers
- scissors • glue or tape
- about 6.5 ft. (2 m) of string

1 Fold one sheet of card stock in half widthwise and open it up. Fold each end into the center to make four folded sections.

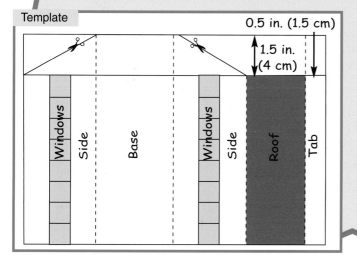

2 Using the template below, cut the folded sheet of card stock as shown and fold along the dotted lines. Draw windows on the sides, and color the roof red. Stick the tab to the opposite side of the card to make the monorail cab.

3 Use the other sheet of card stock to close both open ends of the cab. Cut out the shapes, leaving tabs at the top and bottom. Draw some windows. Stick the shapes to the back and front of the cab.

4 Cut two 2 x 3 in. (5 x 7 cm) card stock rectangles. Fold them in half and then fold back the open ends. Stick them to the cab roof and thread the string through. Tie the string to a cupboard handle and pull the other end tight. Lift and lower the string and watch the cab run up and down the monorail.

Template

0.5 in. (1.5 cm)

1.5 in. (4 cm)

Windows | Side | Base | Windows | Side | Roof | Tab

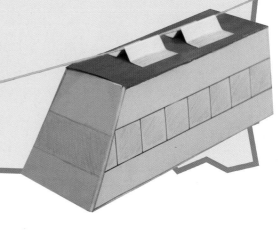

13

Water Transportation

Ships and boats sail from **port** to port across the sea and along rivers and canals. **Cargo** ships carry enormous loads from one side of the world to another.

Small Boats

Narrowboats carry goods and people up and down man-made waterways called canals. Yachts and rowing boats are used for sports and fun. Small fishing boats bring local fish from the sea back to shore.

Yachts with colorful sails compete in a race on calm sea near the coast.

Cranes unload containers from this ship to be transported inland.

Big Boats

Modern **passenger liners** carry vacationers on cruises. They stop at ports for sightseeing along the way. Giant **tankers** carry liquids, such as water or oil, across the oceans. Container ships carry big boxes packed with goods to ports around the world.

Transport Goods Around the World!

Try this card game with a friend.

You will need:
- large sheet of card stock
- scissors • pencil and markers

1 Cut the card stock into 20 playing-card-sized rectangles. Divide the cards into five sets of four and draw (or label) the following on the cards:

Set 1: Dubai, Sydney, oil, oil tanker
Set 2: Miami, the Caribbean, tourists, cruise liner
Set 3: Osaka, Mumbai, computers, container ship
Set 4: Vladivostok, Portsmouth, timber, cargo ship
Set 5: Vancouver, Lima, grain, bulk carrier

2 Shuffle the cards and deal five each. Keep your cards hidden from your opponent.

3 Spread the remaining ten cards face down on a table. The object of the game is to get a complete set of four cards so you have the correct ship to move your cargo from port to port. Check the map to see which cards go together.

4 Take turns picking up a card from the table. Turn it over to show your opponent. If you would like the card, take it and replace it with one from your hand (face down). Otherwise, turn the card back over. Try to remember where the cards are on the table. The first to get a complete set is the winner!

15

Air Transportation

Airplanes carry passengers and their luggage and goods from airport to airport through the sky. The pilot follows a particular flight path so the skies are safe to cross.

Airports

Airports have terminal buildings where passengers and luggage are loaded on and off aircraft. They have long runways for takeoff and landing. **Air traffic control** keeps the airways safe by guiding the aircraft nearby.

Jumbo Jets

Jumbo jets can carry hundreds of passengers on long journeys to far-away places. If all the seats are full, the price of the tickets can be kept lower. It also means fewer flights are made, so less fuel is used.

Jumbo jets travel a long way to foreign countries.

Make a Model Airplane

Ask an adult to help you with this activity.

You will need:
- large sheet of card stock
- pencil • scissors • paint

1 Copy the shapes onto the card stock, using the template as a guide. Cut them out. Ask an adult to help you cut slits along the dotted lines in the body of the airplane.

3 Paint the parts of your airplane and let them dry. Use photographs in books or on the Internet to help you create an airline logo of your own.

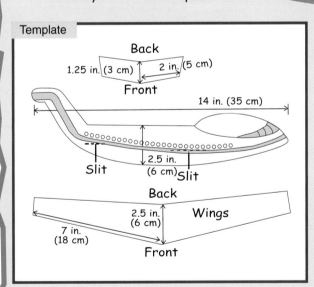

Template

Back
1.25 in. (3 cm)   2 in. (5 cm)
Front

14 in. (35 cm)

Slit   2.5 in. (6 cm) Slit

Back
2.5 in. (6 cm)   Wings
7 in. (18 cm)
Front

4 Find out how many of your classmates have traveled by air. Record your findings on a chart. Where did they go? What kind of aircraft did they fly in?

Destination	Aircraft
Washington D.C.	Boeing 737
Alaska	Helicopter
England	Boeing 757

2 Push the tail and the wings through the slits in the body to make your airplane.

Downtown Traffic

The roads in cities can be very busy. People make local trips or drive through the city as they go from place to place. A road called a **bypass** takes traffic away from the city.

Park and Ride

Many cities have a "park and ride" setup. Visitors can leave their cars in big parking lots in the suburbs and take a bus ride into the city. This keeps the roads less busy and the city cleaner, with fewer **exhaust fumes** in the air.

People are taking this bus into the city instead of using their cars.

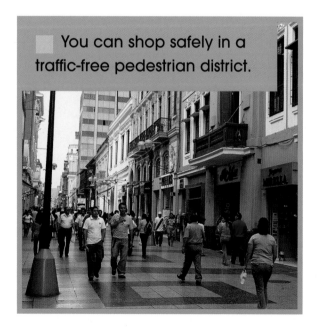

You can shop safely in a traffic-free pedestrian district.

No Traffic Allowed!

Some cities have turned their main shopping areas into **pedestrian districts** where no vehicles are allowed. People can shop without watching for traffic. Other cities have bicycle lanes or bus lanes, which only bicycles or buses are allowed to use.

Plan a Traffic Route

Help keep traffic out of downtown.

You will need:
• pencil • paper
• markers or crayons

1 Copy the map shown below, or make one of your own. You could include a city with houses, shops, surrounding roads, a river, and countryside.

2 Draw in a "park and ride" route. Where will it go? Will you need to build a new road or bridge?

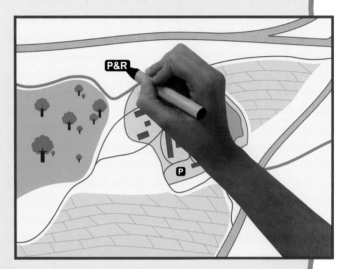

3 Choose a route between the "park and ride" and the city. Color it green.

4 Add a traffic-free pedestrian district close to some shops. Color it yellow.

5 Draw a new bypass to make the roads in the city center less busy.

Explain the route you've chosen for your "park and ride" route. How will your plans affect the natural environment?

Farmland		☩ Church	
Highway		Nature Reserve	
P Parking		Forest	
Houses		Lake	
Shops		River	
P&R Park and Ride		Road	

Private or Public?

Many of the journeys we take are short, local trips. We can travel by private transportation, using our own cars or bicycles, or we can use public transportation, such as trains, buses, and trams.

Private Transportation

Private cars carry people around. Vans and trucks carry work equipment and make local deliveries. Sometimes, motorcycles are used to deliver packages or take-out meals. Cyclists ride their bikes for fresh air and exercise.

This van driver is delivering a box of vegetables to a customer's house.

Public Transportation

When people travel by public transportation, such as buses, trams, and trains, they reduce the number of vehicles used. People buy tickets for their trip, and they are picked up and dropped off along a route.

Trams are a good way to take a short trip into town.

Do a Local Traffic Survey

Ask an adult to help you with this activity.

You will need:
• notebook • pencil

1 With an adult, count the traffic at a spot near you at different times of day.

2 Make two charts, like the ones here, to record your findings.

Which kind of vehicle do you see the most?
Which kind of vehicle do you see the least?

Traffic	Morning	Afternoon
Bicycle	IIII	HHII
Motorcycle	III	II
Car	HHIII	HHI
Van	IIII	II
Truck	IIII	I
Bus	III	HH

3 You may be able to guess what kind of trip a vehicle is making. Can you see children with backpacks in a car, or a delivery van, for example?

Type of Trip	Morning	Afternoon
Going to/ from work	HH	II
Going to/ from school	HHII	HHIII
Shopping	IIII	HHI
Delivery	HHIII	IIII
Pleasure	II	III

What is the most common type of trip?

What is the least common type of trip?

Long Journeys

People take long journeys when they go on vacation, or visit friends or family who live far away. Long journeys are also taken for work trips and delivering goods.

Planning a Journey

Long journeys need careful planning. If you are going by car, you need to plan the route using a map or the Internet. If the trip is going to take more than a day, you need to find somewhere to stay. Tickets must be booked for a trip by plane, boat, or train.

Choosing a Route

When you plan a trip, there may be several different ways of getting there and back. People choose how they travel for lots of different reasons. They may want a fast trip, cheap tickets, a planet-friendly journey, or one that lets them enjoy the beautiful scenery.

On a train trip, you can sit and look at the view.

Plan a Long Journey

1 Choose where you want to go and find it on a map. Is your destination in the same or another state or province?

2 Decide why you are going there—to visit someone, to visit a place, or to go on vacation?

3 Use the Internet to find out how far away your destination is.

4 Choose how you will to get there—car, bus, train, boat, or plane? If you go by:

• **car** – plot your route on a map.

• **train** – which station will you depart from? Where will you arrive?

• **air** – which airport will you depart from? Are there any layovers on the way? Where will you arrive?

• **water** – which port will you depart from? Where will you arrive? What kind of boat will you travel in?

Describe why you have chosen your method of transportation and your destination. For example:

I am going to Washington, D.C., by airplane. It's the fastest way to get there. I really want to visit the White House. We can also see the Lincoln Memorial.

Drive to Kansas City International Airport in Missouri (15 minutes)
Fly from Kansas City, MO to Washington, D.C. (2.5 hours)
Arrive at Ronald Reagan Washington National Airport
Take a taxi to hotel (10 minutes)

Staying Safe

There are rules of the road, air, and water for drivers, pilots, and passengers to follow. They help to prevent accidents and keep travelers safe as they travel from place to place.

On the Road

Drivers must obey speed limits for safety. In towns and cities, low speed limits protect pedestrians. Signs, lights, and markings on the road give safety instructions. Drivers and passengers must always wear seat belts.

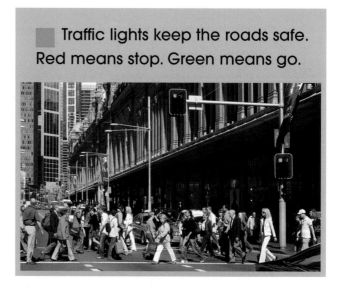

■ Traffic lights keep the roads safe. Red means stop. Green means go.

■ This flight attendant is giving instructions about what to do on an airplane in an emergency.

Safety Instructions

On some journeys, passengers are asked to listen to safety instructions or to read a pamphlet. They learn how to stay safe during a trip, and what to do in case of an accident. There are lifeboats and life jackets aboard a ship. Passengers can pull a cord or handle to stop a train in case of an emergency.

Design a Traffic Safety Leaflet

Design a safety leaflet for drivers, bikers, and adults and children walking to and from your school.

Get to school safely!

Here are some safety instructions you could include:

Drivers
- Don't park near our school gates.
- Drive slowly past our school.
- Don't reverse or turn near our school.

Children
- Always cross the road at the crosswalk.
- Don't walk in the road or near the edge of the sidewalk.
- Look and listen for cars, bicycles, and other vehicles.

Bikers
- Stick to the bike lanes.
- Wear a helmet.
- Look and listen for pedestrians.
- Give clear hand signals.

Stick to the bike lanes.

Always cross the road at the crosswalk.

Planet-Friendly Travel

Transportation can harm the planet. Vehicles burning fuel send exhaust fumes into the air that make it dirty. They also help heat up the planet, which can lead to **global warming**.

Saving Energy

Walking and biking are good ways to get fit and healthy. These forms of transportation are also **eco-friendly**. We use our own **energy**, so no gas or diesel is burned. Traveling by bus or train saves fuel because one vehicle can carry lots of people at a time.

Walking is an eco-friendly way to travel to school.

Eco-Cars

New cars are being designed that are kinder to the planet. Cars can be adapted to run on **biofuel** instead of gas made from oil. Electric cars run on batteries and don't send out exhaust fumes. Soon, cars with **solar panels** may be made to use the sun's energy.

An electric car is recharged, instead of filling it up with gas.

Design an Eco-Friendly Vehicle

1 Design a planet-friendly vehicle for the future. Use the example on the right for ideas.

- How many people will it carry?
- What kind of fuel or power does it run on?
- What is it made of?
- Is it clean or will it send out fumes?

2 Draw and label your design (right). Can you make a model of your design from everyday materials?

Example

A sports car has been made from plant fibers—the body from potato fibers, the seat from soybeans, and the steering wheel from carrot fibers. Its fuel is a mixture of vegetable oil and chocolate. Fumes are cleaned before they go into the air.

Body made of recycled plant materials

Battery charged by electricity from solar panel

Cleaned fumes enter air

Space for seats in the back

Glossary

air traffic control

Air traffic control is a service that makes sure aircraft take off and land safely.

biofuel

Biofuel is a type of fuel made from plants.

border control

Border control is where traffic is checked at a country's border.

bypass

A bypass is a road that carries traffic around a town or city instead of through its center.

cargo

Cargo is the goods carried by trains, trucks, aircraft, and ships.

diesel

Diesel is a type of fuel made from petroleum (oil).

eco-friendly

Things that are eco-friendly do less harm to the planet than things that are not eco-friendly.

electricity

Electricity is a type of energy we use to make things work.

energy

Energy is the power that makes things work. Gas gives vehicles the energy to move.

exhaust fumes

Exhaust fumes are gases sent into the air by vehicles that burn fuel.

global warming

Global warming is the rise in the Earth's temperature. It is partly caused by burning fuels such as gas and diesel.

goods

Goods are items transported by trains, trucks, aircraft, and ships, such as coal or food.

gorge

A gorge is a deep, narrow valley carved out of rocks by a river.

jumbo jet

A jumbo jet is a large aircraft with a wide body that can carry lots of passengers or very big loads.

locomotive

A locomotive is the part of a train containing the engine. It pulls the rest of the train along the tracks.

magnetism

Magnetism is a force that attracts objects made of metal, such as iron.

materials

Materials are what things are made of. Cotton, iron, and wood are all types of materials.

narrowboat

A boat made less than 7 ft. (2.1 m) wide so it can travel on narrow canals.

passenger liner

A passenger liner is a large ship that carries passengers across the sea from port to port or on vacation cruises.

pedestrian district

A pedestrian district is an area in a town with shops for people to walk around. Most vehicles are banned from entering.

port

A port is a place by the coast or a riverbank where boats can load and unload people and goods.

solar panel

A solar panel collects energy from the sun to heat water or to make electricity. In the future, cars could be powered by solar panels.

tanker

A tanker is a truck or a ship designed to carry liquids, such as milk or oil.

traffic

Traffic is the number of cars and other vehicles on a road.

Index